SilverTip

The Rise and Fall of
Ancient Rome

by D. R. Faust

Consultant: Caitlin Krieck, Social Studies Teacher and Instructional Coach, The Lab School of Washington

BEARPORT
PUBLISHING

Minneapolis, Minnesota

T0413508

Credits

Cover and title page, © Iakov Kalinin/Shutterstock; 5, © Viacheslav Lopatin/Shutterstock; 6, © ZU_09/ iStock; 7, © AridOcean/Shutterstock; 9, © Penta Springs Limited/Alamy Stock Photo; 11, © Chronicle/ Alamy Stock Photo; 13, © mikroman6/Getty Images; 15, © DEA / ICAS94/Getty Images; 17, © Pictures from History /Getty Images; 19, © pseudolongino/Shutterstock; 20, © Elena Elisseeva/Shutterstock; 21, © Tonino69/iStock; 25, © ZU_09/iStock; 27, © Pixel-Shot/Shutterstock; 28A, © Viacheslav Lopatin/ Shutterstock; 28B, © Chronicle/Alamy Stock Photo; 28C, © pseudolongino/Shutterstock; 28D, © Tonino69/iStock; 28E, © ZU_09/iStock.

Bearport Publishing Company Product Development Team

President: Jen Jenson; Director of Product Development: Spencer Brinker; Managing Editor: Allison Juda; Associate Editor: Naomi Reich; Associate Editor: Tiana Tran; Art Director: Colin O'Dea; Designer: Kim Jones; Designer: Kayla Eggert; Product Development Assistant: Owen Hamlin

Statement on Usage of Generative Artificial Intelligence

Bearport Publishing remains committed to publishing high-quality nonfiction books. Therefore, we restrict the use of generative AI to ensure accuracy of all text and visual components pertaining to a book's subject. See BearportPublishing.com for details.

Library of Congress Cataloging-in-Publication Data

Names: Faust, Daniel R., author.
Title: The rise and fall of ancient Rome / by D.R. Faust.
Description: Minneapolis, Minnesota : Bearport Publishing Company, [2025] |
   Series: Ancient civilizations : need to know | Includes bibliographical
   references and index.
Identifiers: LCCN 2023059718 (print) | LCCN 2023059719 (ebook) | ISBN
   9798892320450 (library binding) | ISBN 9798892325196 (paperback) | ISBN
   9798892321785 (ebook)
Subjects: LCSH: Rome--History--Juvenile literature. |
   Rome--Civilization--Juvenile literature.
Classification: LCC DG77 .F38 2025 (print) | LCC DG77 (ebook) | DDC
   937--dc23/eng/20240213
LC record available at https://lccn.loc.gov/2023059718
LC ebook record available at https://lccn.loc.gov/2023059719

For more information, write to Bearport Publishing, 5357 Penn Avenue South, Minneapolis, MN 55419.

Contents

Ancient Rome Remains

Everywhere you look in Rome, Italy, there are signs of a long history. You can spot ancient **architecture** in the modern city. Some of its bridges are thousands of years old. These are clues that the city was once the center of a powerful ancient **civilization**.

Many buildings from ancient Rome had arches. These curved shapes can hold a lot of weight. They were often made with extra-strong concrete that used volcanic ash.

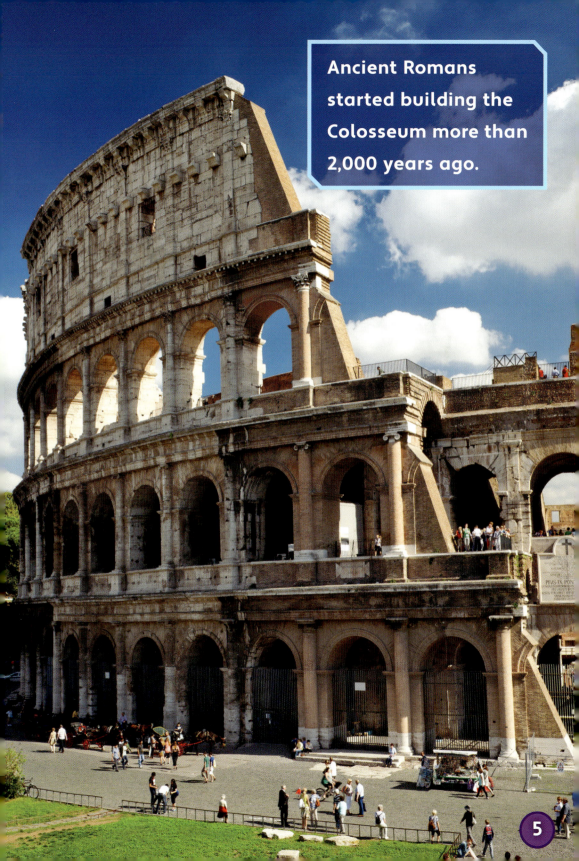

Ancient Romans started building the Colosseum more than 2,000 years ago.

The Founding of Rome

Ancient Rome began in what is modern-day Italy. People started to gather along the Tiber River around 1,000 BCE. They set up small farms and raised animals.

Over time, the settlements grew into cities. The city of Rome was founded in 753 BCE.

Legends say twins Romulus and Remus started Rome. In the stories, Romulus became Rome's first king after killing his brother. The city was named after him.

King Romulus

Tiber River

Rome

Adriatic Sea

Mediterranean Sea

The Roman civilization was not the only one in Italy at the time. The Etruscans (i-TRUHS-kuhnz) and Sabines (SUH-beenz) controlled parts of the land, too. The ancient Greeks had **colonies** along the southern coast.

As the city grew, the Romans took over these other lands. Sometimes, they used force to do so.

The Etruscans once controlled a large part of Italy. After Rome took over, Etruscan culture remained. The ancient Romans made art like the Etruscans. They copied Etruscan architecture.

It's Good to Be King

At first, the civilization was ruled by a line of kings. This time was called the **regal** period.

Roman kings were very powerful and ruled for life. They were the heads of both the government and religion. A group of men called the Senate gave the kings advice.

Each king picked 300 men to join his Senate. Although they were part of the government, members of the Senate had very little power. Kings could do whatever they wanted.

11

The Roman Republic

Rome's regal period came to an end with Tarquin the Proud. He was such a harsh ruler that the people fought back. They removed Tarquin from power in 509 BCE. Then, they formed a new government. This was the beginning of the Roman **Republic**.

A republic is a type of government where people vote for who they want to run the government. These leaders represent the people. They make laws for everyone to follow.

Tarquin the Proud

The new Roman Republic did not have a king. Instead, two consuls were at the top of the government. These leaders were elected to serve for one year. They shared power equally. Like the kings before them, the consuls had a Senate.

Not everyone in the Roman Republic had the right to vote. At first, only wealthy Roman men could vote. They were also the only ones who could be consuls and senators.

Roman consuls

Beyond Italy

Rome's powerful army helped the civilization become a major power of the ancient world. The Roman Republic grew. It began to take over lands beyond Italy.

Ancient Rome spread across the Mediterranean Sea. It **conquered** Greece and parts of northern Africa.

Carthage was a powerful city in northern Africa. It fought Rome over control of the Mediterranean. The two civilizations battled in the Punic Wars from 264 BCE to 146 BCE. Rome's win gave it power over the region.

Carthage General Hannibal led his army over mountains on their way into Italy.

Civil War to Empire

The Roman Republic didn't just fight its neighbors. Sometimes, Romans fought one another. Roman general Julius Caesar waged a war against the Senate from 49 BCE until 45 BCE. When Caesar won, he named himself **dictator** of Rome. This marked the end of the republic.

Julius Caesar ruled Rome like a king. Many grew angry about his new control. Even those in Caesar's government were worried about his power.

Julius Caesar

Political rivals murdered Caesar in 44 BCE. His death led to another struggle for power.

In 27 BCE, Caesar's nephew Octavian became the new ruler. He changed his name to Augustus Caesar and gave himself the title of emperor. This marked the start of the Roman Empire.

Under Augustus Caesar, the Roman Empire continued to grow. As it did, the army built roads, bridges, and towns. Many of them are still around today.

Augustus
Caesar

The Fall of Rome

Eventually, the Romans came to rule most of the known world. But Rome's great power became its downfall. The empire had gotten too large. It took a long time to get information across the wide-reaching lands. This made it difficult to govern. It was also hard to protect all this land.

At its peak, the Roman Empire stretched across large parts of Europe. It held land in western Asia and northern Africa. All of this land was ruled by the emperor.

ASIA

EUROPE

Atlantic
Ocean

Mediterranean Sea

Roman Empire

AFRICA

As it was growing, the Roman Empire made enemies. Civilizations fought to stay free. Others wanted control over some of the empire's land.

The **Germanic** Visigoths (VIZ-uh-*gahths*) attacked Rome in 410 CE. Then in 476 CE, warrior Odoacer took over the city with his troops. This ended the Roman Empire.

After the Roman Empire fell, Europe broke apart into smaller kingdoms. Many would go on to become countries we still see today. Spain, France, and Great Britain all came out of this divide.

Odoacer

Laws and Language

The ancient Roman civilization ended more than 1,500 years ago. But it still impacts our lives today. Many modern languages came from Latin. This was the language spoken by the Romans. Today's governments and laws are a lot like those in ancient Rome. It may be gone, but it's not forgotten.

More than 2,000 years ago, the Romans made a 12-month calendar. They broke each day into 24 hours. We still use this calendar and clock today.

Ancient Rome Timeline

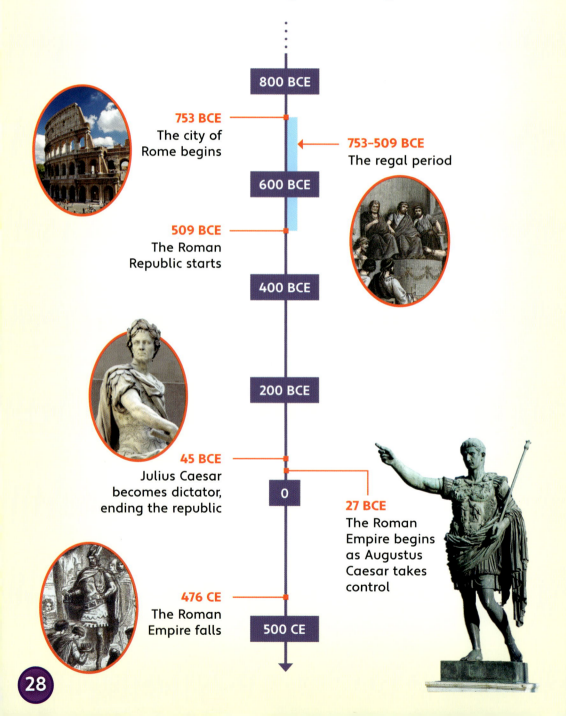

800 BCE

753 BCE
The city of
Rome begins

753–509 BCE
The regal period

600 BCE

509 BCE
The Roman
Republic starts

400 BCE

200 BCE

45 BCE
Julius Caesar
becomes dictator,
ending the republic

0

27 BCE
The Roman
Empire begins
as Augustus
Caesar takes
control

476 CE
The Roman
Empire falls

500 CE

★ SilverTips for REVIEW

Review what you've learned. Use the text to help you.

Define key terms

consul   Roman Republic

regal period   Senate

Roman Empire

Check for understanding

Describe the way the government worked during the Roman Republic.

How did Julius Caesar change ancient Rome?

Why did the Roman Empire fall?

Think deeper

How has the culture and civilization of ancient Rome impacted your life today?

★ SilverTips on TEST-TAKING

- **Make a study plan.** Ask your teacher what the test is going to cover. Then, set aside time to study a little bit every day.

- **Read all the questions carefully.** Be sure you know what is being asked.

- **Skip any questions** you don't know how to answer right away. Mark them and come back later if you have time.

Glossary

architecture a style or method of building

civilization a large group of people who share the same history and way of life

colonies areas that have been settled by people from another country and are ruled by that country

conquered took control through the use of force

dictator a person who has complete control over a country

empire a large region ruled by a single person or government

Germanic from a part of the world where German is spoken

legends stories handed down from long ago that are often based on some facts but cannot be proven

regal relating to a king or kings

republic a government where individuals are elected to represent groups of people

Read More

Andrews, Elizabeth. *The Ancient Romans (Ancient Civilizations).* Minneapolis: Pop!, 2023.

Mather, Charis. *The Peculiar Past in Ancient Rome (Strange History).* Minneapolis: Bearport Publishing Company, 2024.

Reynolds, Donna. *Ancient Rome Revealed (Unearthing Ancient Civilizations).* New York: Cavendish Square Publishing, 2023.

Learn More Online

1. Go to **www.factsurfer.com** or scan the QR code below.

2. Enter "**Civilizations Ancient Rome**" into the search box.

3. Click on the cover of this book to see a list of websites.

Index

About the Author

D. R. Faust is a freelance writer of fiction and nonfiction. They live in Queens, NY.